HOW
AIRPLANES
WORK

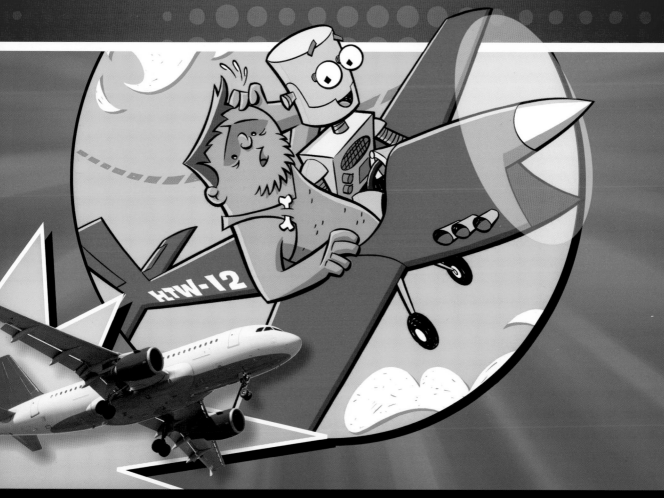

HTW-12

BY PAUL D. GUMANN · ILLUSTRATED BY GLEN M...

The Child's World®

Published by The Child's World®
1980 Lookout Drive • Mankato, MN 56003-1705
800-599-READ • www.childsworld.com

ACKNOWLEDGMENTS
The Child's World®: Mary Berendes, Publishing Director
Content Consultant: Adam Green, PhD, Associate Professor
  of Physics, University of St. Thomas
The Design Lab: Design and production
Red Line Editorial: Editorial direction

LIBRARY OF CONGRESS
CATALOGING-IN-PUBLICATION DATA
Ohmann, Paul.
  How airplanes work / by Paul R. Ohmann ;
illustrated by Glen Mullaly.
    p. cm.
  Includes bibliographical references and index.
  ISBN 978-1-60973-213-4 (library reinforced : alk. paper)
  1. Airplanes--Juvenile literature. I. Mullaly, Glen, 1968- ill.
  II. Title.
  TL547.O36 2012
  629.132--dc22   2011010912

Photo Credits © iStockphoto, cover, 1, 7 (bottom), 11; Bain
News Service/Library of Congress, 4 (left), 5 (right); Library
of Congress, 4 (right), 5 (left), 6; John T. Daniels/AP Images,
7 (top); AP Images, 8; Dave Barnard/Shutterstock Images,
13; Shutterstock Images, 20; Rostislav Glinsky/Shutterstock
Images, 28

Printed in the United States of America in Mankato,
Minnesota.
July 2011
PA02092

ABOUT THE AUTHOR

Paul R. Ohmann is thrilled to write his first children's book. He has a doctorate in physics from the University of Wisconsin-Madison and is currently an associate professor of physics at the University of St. Thomas in St. Paul, Minnesota. In addition to science, Paul enjoys traveling and eating ethnic foods, especially with his wife and son.

ABOUT THE ILLUSTRATOR

Glen Mullaly draws neato pictures for kids of all ages from his swanky studio on the west coast of Canada. He lives with his awesomely understanding wife and their spectacularly indifferent cat. Glen loves old books, magazines, and cartoons, and someday wants to illustrate a book on How Monsters Work!

TABLE OF CONTENTS

CHAPTER ONE 4

CHAPTER TWO 9

CHAPTER THREE 19

CHAPTER FOUR 30

WORDS TO KNOW • FIND OUT MORE • INDEX 32

WE HAVE LIFTOFF!

This is way better than riding a pterodactyl!

"Fasten your seatbelts, and put your chairs in the upright position," the flight attendant announces over the loud speakers.

The tall man ahead of you shifts his seat forward. You can finally move your legs. The flight attendants walk down the aisles making sure everyone is ready for takeoff.

The engines begin to roar. The airplane starts rolling down the runway. It moves faster and faster. You

TIME LINE

1485
Leonardo da Vinci designs a flying machine, the ornithopter.

1783
Jean François Pilâtre de Rozier and Marquis d'Arlandes make the first trip in a hot air balloon.

1785
Jean-Pierre Blanchard and John Jeffries cross the English Channel in a hot air balloon.

1852
Henri Giffard's steam-powered airship makes its first flight. The airship is similar to a blimp.

glance out the window. The scenery becomes a blur. You feel when the plane first leaves the ground. Soon, your seat is at an angle facing up toward the sky. The plane rises higher and higher in the air.

You look down and see cars, streets, and rooftops. They're so tiny they seem like toys. Flying is so cool! Eventually, your seat levels off a bit. You grab your crossword puzzle to work on during the long flight. Yet you can't help but wonder: How do airplanes work? What makes them fly? Where did the first airplanes come from?

1891
Otto Lilienthal makes the first controlled flight from a glider. The glider is a forerunner to the modern hang glider.

1903
The Wright brothers make the first controlled, powered flight in a manned flying machine.

1914
Fighter planes are built for use in World War I.

1927
Charles Lindbergh makes the first solo flight across the Atlantic Ocean.

Traveling on airplanes had been becoming popular since the 1930s. Now people wanted to go farther and get there faster. In 1949, the first jet airliner was built. It was the British De Havilland DH-106 Comet. The plane could fly at speeds of more than 500 miles per hour (805 km/h).

Orville and Wilbur Wright built the first working airplane. The Wright brothers flew it in Kitty Hawk, North Carolina, on December 17, 1903. On the plane's first flight, Orville flew for 12 seconds. He covered a distance of 120 feet (37 m). Later that day, Wilbur flew 852 feet (260 m) in 59 seconds. There were no extra passengers on these flights, though.

1936
American Airlines uses the Douglas DC-3. It is the first successful passenger airplane.

1947
Charles Yeager flies the first plane faster than the speed of sound, which is 1,116 feet per second (340 m/s) at sea level.

1957
The Soviet Union sends the first satellite, *Sputnik I*, into space.

The first airplane passenger was Charles Furnas. He was a mechanic who flew with one of the Wrights in 1908.

Wilbur Wright watches as Orville Wright flies the brothers' plane in 1903.

1962
John H. Glenn Jr. is the first person to orbit Earth in a spacecraft.

2000
Astronauts begin to live in the International Space Station that orbits Earth.

TODAY
Airplanes and airports can be found in cities around the world. About 55 million passengers fly on planes each day.

In the 1480s, Leonardo da Vinci began trying to figure out if flight was possible. He created a design for a flying machine called an ornithopter. It had wings that would flap like a bird's. His machine was never built, though.

A man tests a type of ornithopter in 1932.

Airplane travel is as popular as ever. People can cross the globe in a matter of hours. As technology continues to develop, aircraft keep getting bigger and faster.

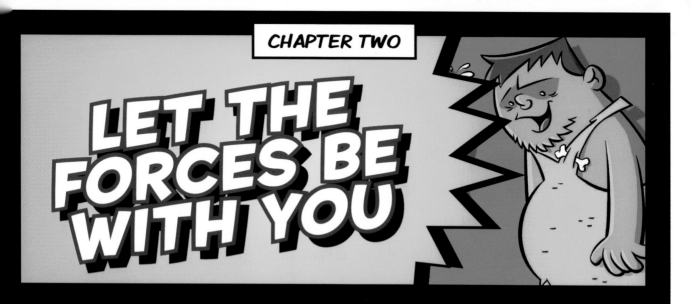

CHAPTER TWO

LET THE FORCES BE WITH YOU

Before understanding how airplanes work, you first have to understand air. It's easy to ignore air because we can walk, talk, and see right through it. But air is all around us. We breathe it, and on windy days, we can feel it.

So, to understand airplanes, think of air as a *thing* or as *stuff*. Air is a fluid—stuff that flows easily. A fluid can be a liquid, like water, or a gas, like air. Air flows in the form of wind.

You're hopeless.

Air is a fluid, so I'm going swimming!

Thinking of air as a fluid will help you understand how airplanes fly. Air flows around the airplane. It applies strong forces that let the airplane to take off, turn, change **altitude**, and land. The two most important forces for flight are called **thrust** and **lift**. They must be stronger than the forces of **drag** and **gravity** to keep the plane flying easily. Let's look at these four forces one at a time to see how they work together (or against each other) when a plane flies.

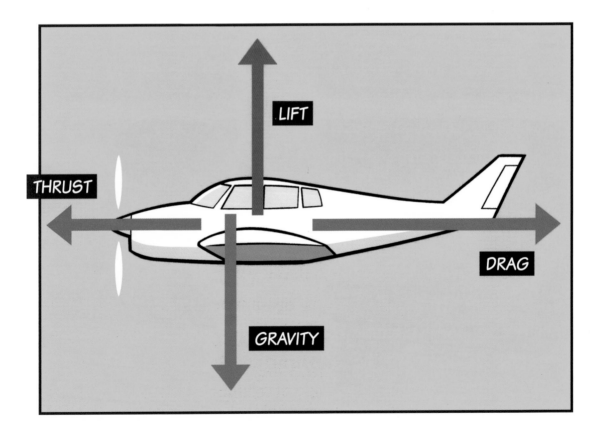

1. Thrust

The force that pushes an airplane forward is called thrust. All airplanes are powered by spinning blades. Sometimes they are part of a propeller. Sometimes they're inside an engine.

Blades spin inside a jet engine.

An airplane's spinning blades create thrust by pulling air from the front of the plane and making it quickly flow backward. By pushing air backward, the plane is pushed forward. The same thing happens when you swim. You push water backward, and your body moves forward. The moving water gives your body thrust. The harder and faster you push, the faster you swim. For an airplane, the faster the blades spin, the greater the thrust. The greater the thrust, the faster the airplane moves.

HOW DO PROPELLERS WORK?

The key to a propeller is its shape. The blades are twisted more toward the inside than they are at the tips. Take a look at a fan in your house. Its blades might be shaped like this, too. As a propeller spins, the twisted part on the inside scoops up air. The air then moves along the blade to the flatter tip, where it is pushed back. Scooping air and pushing it backward creates thrust. The amount of thrust depends on the speed of the propeller and the curve of the blades.

When you go swimming, the motion of your hands serves the same purpose as an airplane's propeller. First, you reach forward to scoop some water. Then you move your hand backward to push the water behind you. Your hand and arm twist to create thrust.

2. Drag

Have you ridden in a car and stuck your hand out the window? Did you feel the air pushing against it? Did you notice the air push harder as you went faster? If so, then you've felt drag. Drag is the force that resists the motion of an object—in this case, the motion of the car. Drag works against thrust.

A dog feels drag when it sticks its head out the window of a moving car.

WHAT A DRAG!

Have you heard of swimmers shaving their legs? Have you seen downhill skiers crouch low to the ground? Have you seen how race cars are short and flat instead of tall like trucks? These are all things that reduce drag. Even something as minor as the hair on a swimmer's legs can slow the swimmer down just a tiny bit. So swimmers and racers in every sport do their best to reduce drag. The same is true for airplanes. That is why their wheels are raised after takeoff and their wings are very thin. The less drag, the easier it is to go fast.

3. Gravity

You probably know that everything on Earth has weight. Some airplanes weigh more than 800,000 pounds (362,874 kg) at takeoff! Since air is a thing too, it also has weight. It's very, very light, though.

Why is weight important? The more something weighs, the more gravity pulls down on it. The more

gravity pulling down, the harder it is to lift the thing off the ground. That's why a big airplane has several big engines and very big wings. They are needed to overcome the large force of gravity that tries to pull the plane back down to the ground. A smaller plane only needs a small engine and small wings because it has less gravity to overcome.

4. Lift

Lift is the force that holds an airplane in the air. Lift must be stronger than gravity. The key to an airplane's lift is in the design of its wings. Air bends up as it hits the front of the wing. Then the air follows the curve of the wing in a downward direction. This downward bending of air causes the wings, and the entire plane, to lift. In other words, the wing forces the air downward, and the air forces the wing upward.

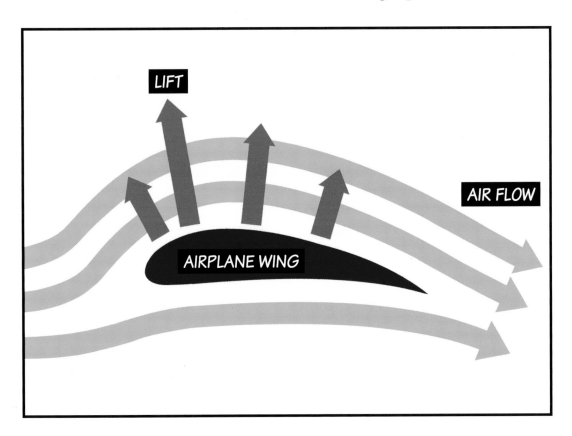

SPOON EXPERIMENT

You can test the idea behind lift by placing a spoon under a water faucet.

1. Hold the end of the spoon handle, and point the spoon downward into the sink. Make sure the spoon is straight up and down.

2. Slowly move the back of the spoon into the stream of water.

3. The water moves along the back of the spoon and then turns in the direction of the inward curve of the spoon. You will feel the spoon being pulled toward the water. This is similar to what happens when air flows around an airplane wing.

4. Also, the faster the water flows around the spoon, the bigger the force on the spoon. The faster the air moves around the plane, the greater the lift.

Slats and Flaps

Wings also have moving parts on them that slightly change the shape of the wings. The moving parts at the front of the wings are called slats. Those at the back of the wings are called flaps. Pilots can adjust the slats and flaps to give an airplane more or less lift.

CHAPTER THREE
FLYING THE PLANE

Now you know about the forces that allow planes to fly. Next, you will see how these forces work in each stage of an airplane's flight. Let's look at takeoff first.

An airplane has to move forward quickly to take off. It needs thrust. Second, it has to go up. It needs lift. In other words, thrust must overcome drag, and lift must overcome gravity. An airplane's blades in the engine or propeller spin faster to increase thrust. Lift increases at the same time. This is because the air is moving more quickly around the wings and through the propellers.

An airplane rises in the air once there is enough thrust and lift.

At takeoff, the pilot also extends the slats and flaps so the plane can get as much lift as possible.

Once the plane is in the air, the nose of the airplane tilts up higher than the back of the plane. This makes the airplane fly higher.

In the Air

A few minutes after takeoff, the airplane reaches its cruising altitude. This is the height that the pilot

WHO MADE THAT PLANE?

It is expensive to design, test, and build airplanes. That is why only two companies make all the big, modern passenger airplanes in the world. The two companies are Boeing Company and Airbus Corporation. How can you tell which company made the plane you're flying on? Boeing makes the airplanes that start and end with a 7, such as the 747. Airbus Corporation makes the planes that start with an A, such as the A320.

chooses to get the best, smoothest ride through the sky. It is where a passenger plane spends most of its flight.

When cruising, the four forces are balanced. In order for the airplane to stay at one height, lift must equal gravity. To stay at one speed, thrust must equal drag. The pilot reduces the airplane's lift and thrust by

CHECK THE TILT!

Ask a flight attendant for a cup of water the next time you are on a plane. Set the cup on your tray. Look carefully at the liquid in it. The water looks tilted. But, the water is actually straight across. It's the glass, you, your seat, and everything else in the plane that is tilted up.

It really works! Did you try it?

slowing down the engines. Lowering the wing flaps and slats helps, too. Also, the airplane tilts downward. But the nose of the plane is still pointed up a little bit. This gives the plane enough lift to keep it from falling. If the nose drops too much, then the lifting force becomes too small, and the plane loses altitude.

What about Steering?

Does an airplane really need the big fins at the end of the tail? You bet it does! The tail keeps a plane from wobbling in the air.

Look closely at the tail. One fin is sideways, like a tabletop. The other is up-and-down, like a sail. Each fin has pieces, called controllers, that the pilot can control from the cockpit.

The controllers on the sideways fin are called elevators. They move the plane up and down. When they tilt upward, the plane's nose also tilts upward. The plane climbs. When the elevators tilt downward, the nose drops and the plane goes down.

The controller on the up-and-down fin is the rudder. If the rudder points to the left, the plane turns to the left.

If the rudder points to the right, the plane turns to the right. The left and right turning motion is called yaw.

A pilot can also turn the plane by using the rudder and two adjustable pieces on the wings. These pieces are ailerons. By raising one aileron and lowering the other, one wing goes down while the other goes up. This is called rolling.

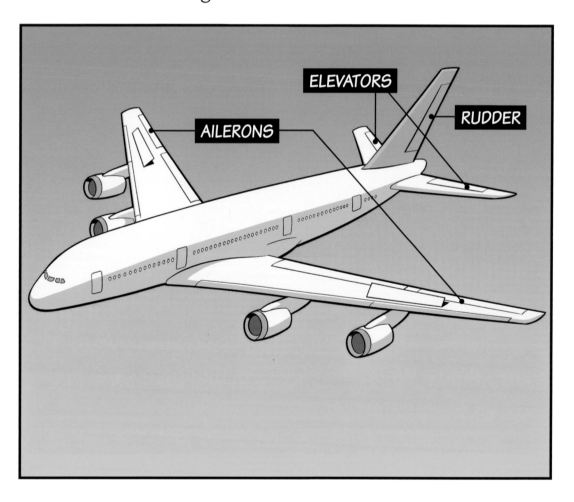

ELEVATORS

RUDDER

AILERONS

AIRPLANE MOVEMENTS

PITCH

ROLL

YAW

Landing

You've learned what a plane needs for takeoff. A plane needs the opposite to land. Drag must be greater than thrust to slow the plane down. Gravity must be greater than lift so the plane can drop.

THE NEED FOR SPEED

If you like fast planes, check out this list of aircraft and their speeds:

AIRPLANE	SPEED
X-43A Scramjet	7,000 miles per hour (11,265 km/h) top speed
North American X-15	4,534 miles per hour (7,297 km/h) top speed
SR-71 Blackbird	2,193 miles per hour (3,529 km/h) top speed
MiG-25 Foxbat	2,110 miles per hour (3,396 km/h) top speed
Boeing 747	640 miles per hour (1,030 km/h) cruising speed

The pilot slows down the engine to decrease the airflow over the wings. This slows the plane down and reduces the lift. A plane extends its slats and flaps as it approaches the runway. This helps ensure that the lift won't decrease too fast. That way, the plane does not lose altitude too quickly.

Just a couple minutes before touching down, the plane begins to level out. The pilot can more easily see

the runway up ahead. The engines slow down even more, creating less thrust, as the plane descends. The pilot controls the rudder, elevators, and ailerons to steady the plane as it lands. These controls are more important if it is windy outside.

Once the plane is on the runway, how does is stop so quickly? If you've been on a plane before, you may have worried the plane is going too fast to stop. For example, a Boeing 747 lands going about 160 miles per hour (257 km/h). But a few seconds later, you felt at ease. The plane stopped. How? A passenger plane uses brakes on the tires to slow down very quickly. Many planes also have spoilers. These are adjustable flaps on the wings that help create more drag. Some airplanes can even thrust in reverse. In other words, air flows forward instead of backward. This slows the plane even more quickly than using only the brakes.

A *pilot controls the plane's rudder, elevators, and ailerons for a smooth landing.*

AIRPLANE SAFETY

Before every flight, an airplane goes through a careful safety check to make sure all systems are working correctly.

Safety features are built into each airplane. At the beginning of a flight, attendants describe the safety equipment to passengers. There are oxygen masks that drop down if the air pressure becomes too low. There are life vests or other flotation devices in case the plane lands in water. There are also emergency exits people can leave the plane through in case of emergency.

The safety equipment hardly ever needs to be used because planes are so safe. But they can save lives if there is an emergency.

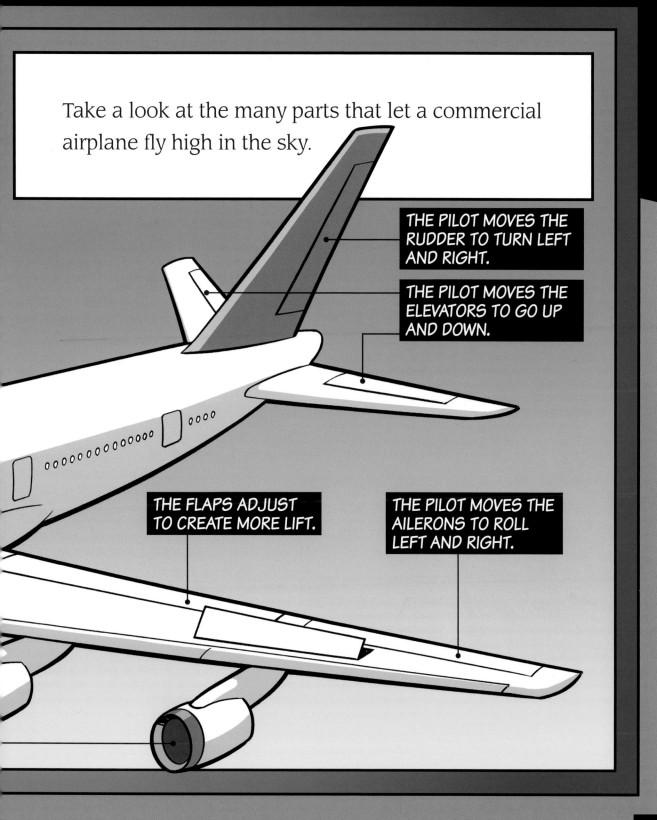

Take a look at the many parts that let a commercial airplane fly high in the sky.

THE PILOT MOVES THE RUDDER TO TURN LEFT AND RIGHT.

THE PILOT MOVES THE ELEVATORS TO GO UP AND DOWN.

THE FLAPS ADJUST TO CREATE MORE LIFT.

THE PILOT MOVES THE AILERONS TO ROLL LEFT AND RIGHT.

WORDS TO KNOW

altitude (AL-tih-tood): Altitude is the height of something above sea level. Once in the air, airplanes usually fly at a steady altitude.

drag (DRAG): Drag is the force that resists the motion of an object. An airplane must overcome drag to move forward.

gravity (GRAV-uh-tee): Gravity is the force that pulls things to the ground and keeps them from floating away into space. An airplane must overcome gravity to lift into the air.

lift (LIFT): Lift is the force that pushes the wings of an airplane upward as a plane moves through the air. An airplane must have lift to rise into the air.

thrust (THRUST): Thrust is the force that moves an object, such as an airplane, forward. An airplane must have thrust to rise into the air.

FIND OUT MORE

Visit our Web site for links about how airplanes work: *childsworld.com/links*

Note to Parents, Teachers, and Librarians: We routinely verify our Web links to make sure they are safe and active sites. So encourage your readers to check them out!

INDEX

ailerons, 24, 27, 31
air, 5, 9–10, 11, 12, 13, 14, 16, 17, 20–21, 23, 28, 29
Airbus Corporation, 21
altitude, 10, 21, 23, 26
blades, 11, 12, 20
Boeing Company, 21
cockpit, 23, 30
da Vinci, Leonardo, 8
drag, 10, 13, 14, 20, 22, 25, 28, 30
elevators, 23, 24, 27, 31

engine, 4, 11, 15, 20, 23, 26, 27, 30
fins, 23
flaps, 18, 21, 23, 26, 28, 31
Furnas, Charles, 7
gravity, 10, 14–15, 16, 20, 22, 25
lift, 10, 15, 16, 17, 18, 20–24, 25, 26, 30, 31
pilot, 4, 18, 21–24, 26–27, 30–31
propeller, 11, 12, 20

rudder, 23–24, 27, 31
slats, 18, 21, 23, 26, 30
spoilers, 28, 30
tail, 23
thrust, 10, 11, 12, 13, 20, 22, 25, 27, 28, 30
wings, 8, 14, 15, 16, 18, 20, 24, 26, 28, 30
Wright brothers, 6–7